◆◆◆◆◆◆◆◆◆◆◆◆◆◆◆◆

Lewis
and Clark

Lewis and Clark

BY
JON NOONAN
ILLUSTRATED BY YOSHI MIYAKE

CRESTWOOD HOUSE
NEW YORK

Maxwell Macmillan Canada
Toronto

Maxwell Macmillan International
New York Oxford Singapore Sydney

To all my friends.

CRESTWOOD HOUSE
Macmillan Publishing Company
866 Third Avenue, New York, NY 10022

Maxwell Macmillan Canada, Inc.
1200 Eglinton Avenue East, Suite 200
Don Mills, Ontario M3C 3N1

Macmillan Publishing Company is part of the
Maxwell Communication Group of Companies

First Edition
Book design by Sylvia Frezzolini
Printed in the United States of America

10 9 8 7 6 5 4 3 2 1

LIBRARY OF CONGRESS CATALOGING-IN-PUBLICATION DATA

Noonan, Jon.
Lewis and Clark / by Jon Noonan. — 1st ed.
p.   cm. — (Explorers)
Includes Index.
Summary: Examines the achievements of the two men who led the great exploring expedition through territory gained by the Louisiana Purchase.
ISBN 0-89686-707-2
1. Lewis and Clark Expedition (1804–1806)—Juvenile literature. 2. Lewis, Meriwether, 1774–1809—Juvenile literature. 3. Clark, William, 1770–1838—Juvenile literature. [1. Lewis, Meriwether, 1774–1809. 2. Clark, William, 1770–1838. 3. Explorers. 4. Lewis and Clark Expedition (1804–1806)] I. Title. II. Series: Noonan, Jon. Explorers.
F592.7.N55   1993   92-9381
917.804'2—dc20

CONTENTS

THE ADVENTURES OF LEWIS AND CLARK

Captain Clark and the Cloudburst

Captain Clark explored the land close to five great waterfalls. As they poured over the cliffs, the beautiful **cascades** filled the air with a tremendous roar.

Searching the ground carefully, Clark hoped to find some special papers he had lost near the tallest waterfall. Carrying her baby son, Sacagawea (sak-a-ja-we-a) and her husband Charbonneau (shar-bon-o) came along to search too.

Captain Lewis and others in their group waited up ahead. At that time in 1805, the Lewis and Clark **expedition** was exploring the Great Falls of the Missouri River in what is now Montana.

These explorers were on a special journey to the Pacific Ocean for Thomas Jefferson, the third president of the young United States of America.

The special papers were some of Clark's notes about their explorations. It was important that their reports be complete. Clark and the Charbonneaus continued to search for them.

All of a sudden as their luck would have it, a stupendous storm came upon the explorers. The clouds burst out with hail and rain. It seemed as though a flood was falling from the sky. The swift wind battered their bodies with ice stones.

Clark and his three companions sought shelter from the storm. They stood under a shelf of rock that stuck out on the side of a **ravine.** Overwhelming amounts of water poured over them.

Up ahead a flash flood suddenly came rushing through the ravine!

The shocked Charbonneau scrambled to the top. Once there Charbonneau extended a helping hand to his wife.

Still standing in the ravine, as the water rose to his chest, Clark first pushed Sacagawea and the baby to safety above the rock shelf. Then Clark climbed up too.

The rising flood tore by, ripping rocks out of the ravine along the way. The water shoved its way into the rapids of the fast-flowing Missouri

River and over a waterfall nearly 100 feet tall.

If they had stayed, the now-15-foot-high wall of water would have washed Clark and the others over the waterfall too. Instead they stood high on a hill, safe on solid ground.

Search for Shoshonis

Before arriving at the Great Falls, Captain Clark and Captain Lewis had been leading their 31 fellow explorers in boats and canoes upstream on the wide Missouri River. All the way from St. Louis, the Missouri River served as their guide across the plains to the Rocky Mountains. The group had not seen a single living soul as they traveled across the future state of Montana. They saw thousands of buffaloes and lots of grizzly bears but no people.

As the gigantic snow-covered Rocky Mountains grew closer the explorers hoped to find some Shoshoni Indians. The two captains wanted to trade for horses and form a peaceful friendship with them. Sacagawea, a Shoshoni, also wished to see them. She had been taken away from her tribe by enemy warriors when she was a girl.

As the storm eased away Clark and the Charbonneau family walked ahead to meet Lewis and the others.

York

The foursome was joined by Clark's servant, York. Although born a slave, he and Clark, a Southerner, had been friends since childhood. Here in the wide American wilderness York found more freedom than he had ever had in his life. Although in the South it was then almost unheard of, Clark let his servant carry a rifle and let him freely leave the group to hunt or do whatever he wished.

This time York had used his freedom to try to find Clark in the storm. Through the flash floods and hailstones York had searched for Clark around the waterfalls. He found Clark and the Charbonneau family just as they climbed to the top of the hill.

The explorers continued toward Captain Lewis's group where the expedition's canoes and boats were waiting. This equipment had been carried around the falls. After finding Lewis, Clark learned that the floods, strong winds and seven-inch-round ice stones had almost killed some of the men.

The Search Goes On

After everyone recovered Captain Clark took his boat ahead with Sacagawea and a small group of men. Still searching for the Shoshonis, they came

to the spot where three rivers flowed into the Missouri River. He and Captain Lewis would call them the Jefferson, Madison and Gallatin rivers. Sacagawea said the Shoshonis should be there.

In this very spot Sacagawea had been taken away five years earlier by Hidatsa Minitari Indians. After killing some Shoshoni warriors the Minitaris took a few Shoshoni women away to be their slaves. Sacagawea was 17 now. She had been only 12 then.

For the next two days Clark and his group walked more than 50 miles around the area looking for the Shoshonis. He came back to Lewis's group after sighting two grizzly bears but no Shoshonis.

After several more days of travel Sacagawea saw a hill, shaped like a beaver's head, that she remembered. She said the Shoshonis would be found on the other side. This time Captain Lewis took a turn to lead a group of **scouts.** He took along three other men.

If there were trouble up ahead the scouting group was supposed to find it first. One of these men, George Drouilliard, was the expedition's best scout and hunter. He was also skilled in the Indian sign language. Everyone called him Drewyer. The other two were Hugh McNeal and John Shields.

The Shoshonis Are Found

Lewis and the scouts found a horse-trodden path that led along a creek. The group split up. Drewyer went into the woods on the right side of the trail. Shields took the left side. Lewis and McNeal walked up the middle.

Then suddenly, through his telescope, Lewis saw one Shoshoni man on horseback. He was coming toward them. He seemed to be alone.

One mile away, the clear-eyed Shoshoni saw Lewis. He halted his horse and sat very still.

Lewis swiftly thought of something to do. He took out a blanket and held it at two corners. Three times he tossed the blanket in the air, spread it out and pulled it to the ground.

This action was a sign of peace among Missouri River Indians. Lewis hoped it would work.

As Lewis waved the blanket Drewyer and Shields continued forward on the sides of the trail.

The Shoshoni man stayed still after Lewis finished. He gave no sign in return. Perhaps he feared a trap was being set. He could see Drewyer and Shields still walking toward him with their rifles close at hand.

Lewis thought a shout to Drewyer and Shields might scare the Shoshoni away. He quickly gave his own rifle to McNeal and pulled some gifts out of his pack. Then, holding the gifts in his hands,

Lewis slowly started to walk toward the Shoshoni man too.

Lewis got as close as 100 paces before the Shoshoni swiftly turned his horse around, leaped across the creek and rode away into the woods.

The scouts stayed to see if other Shoshonis would come. When none did they continued up the trail. The creek grew thinner and thinner. Soon they could stand with a foot on each side of the little waterway. They had reached a small source creek which led into the wide Missouri River.

On the following day they saw a Shoshoni man and two women, then another woman and two girls farther along. As the scouts came closer, every one of them ran away except for a young girl and an elderly woman. They seemed too scared to move.

Since Lewis and his men were dressed in **elk** hides and their light-colored skin had browned after a year in the outdoors, they looked like American Indians. The captain lifted his sleeves to uncover his arms. The woman and girl were surprised. Lewis and his scouts were the first white-skinned people these Shoshonis had ever seen. Then Lewis gave them gifts, surprising them again. The second girl came out of hiding and she was given gifts too.

Walking a little farther Lewis and his scouts got a surprise of their own. Sixty horse-riding Shoshoni warriors, all armed with bows and arrows, came racing toward the four explorers. The warriors had answered the call of the first Shoshoni man who had fled earlier.

Lewis left his gun and walked alone toward the warriors. As he came forward the two girls and the woman spoke to the Shoshoni chief and showed him their gifts. Chief Cameahwait (kam-ee-a-wait) could see that Lewis was generous and wished for peace. The chief and two other Shoshoni warriors stepped toward the captain and gave him a friendly welcome hug. Then all the Shoshonis gave hugs to all the scouts.

After this success Lewis and Drewyer convinced the Shoshonis (using sign language) to come with them to see all the explorers. The Shoshonis were surprised when they saw York for the first time. They had never seen a black-skinned person before either.

When the entire expedition and the Shoshoni village got together, Sacagawea spoke as the **interpreter.** Imagine Sacagawea's joy when first she found a close girlfriend of her childhood and then learned that her brother had become chief of the village. Her brother was Chief Cameahwait! Sacagawea cried tears of happiness.

Several other surprises and adventures were in store for these explorers on their journey across America in the years 1804 to 1806. All the way they were led by the courageous Captains Lewis and Clark.

LEWIS AND CLARK
BEFORE THE EXPEDITION

Lewis and Clark were both born in **colonial** America in the 1770s, a few short years before Thomas Jefferson wrote the Declaration of Independence.

The youngest son in a family of six boys and four girls, William Clark was born in Caroline County, Virginia, on August 1, 1770. The oldest son in a family of three boys and two girls, Meriwether Lewis was born in nearby Albemarle County, Virginia, on August 18, 1774.

At one time the Lewis and Clark families lived close to the lands of Thomas Jefferson in Albemarle County and became his friends. The Clarks moved to Caroline County before William was born however. The Lewises stayed in Albemarle

County and as he grew up, Meriwether became a friend of Thomas Jefferson.

When Meriwether was almost five, his father died and his mother remarried the following year. When he was seven the family moved to the woodlands of Georgia but they returned to Albemarle County when Meriwether was 14.

When William was 15 in 1785, his family moved down the Ohio River to live in Kentucky.

Officers

Meriwether Lewis's father and stepfather and all of William Clark's brothers had been officers or soldiers during the American Revolution. One of William's brothers, George Rogers Clark, became especially famous for his bravery and skill in combat.

As soon as they could, as teenagers, Clark and Lewis became soldiers too. They joined the U.S. Army and soon became officers. They served for several years on the frontier lands of the United States. Lewis and Clark were used to guns and hunting since childhood. In early 1796 they became members of the same "Chosen Rifle Company" which William Clark commanded.

That summer Clark left the army as a first lieutenant and went home to Kentucky. Lewis stayed and rose in rank to captain. One day in 1801 Captain Lewis received a letter from the president of the United States.

For a long time Thomas Jefferson had wondered what the land west of the young United States was like. In 1792, 18-year-old Meriwether Lewis volunteered to explore the West for him. At that time Jefferson was the secretary of state for President George Washington. Jefferson thought Lewis was too young then.

In 1801 however, when Jefferson became president of the United States, he thought of Lewis again. He chose Lewis to be his personal secretary and Lewis accepted.

LEWIS AND CLARK
ARE CHOSEN

In 1803 Jefferson decided Lewis was ready to lead an exploration of the West. The expedition would search for water routes going all the way to the Pacific Ocean. The president asked Lewis to choose a co-commander. That summer Lewis asked Clark. With Jefferson's approval he said Clark would become a captain too. Clark felt ready for new adventures. Eagerly, he said yes.

In that same year the sale of the Louisiana Purchase from France to the United States was completed. Now almost a million square miles of land was added to the western boundary of the young nation. Exploring across this territory and onward to the Pacific Ocean became especially important to Jefferson.

The First Camp

Lewis and Clark set up their expedition's first camp close to St. Louis. They called it Camp Wood. At that time St. Louis was a village on the edge of the American frontier. In the future St. Louis would become a large city in Missouri and a gigantic arch would be built to honor the location as the gateway to the West.

At Camp Wood Lewis and Clark prepared for their long journey. They added to their supplies and trained their company. In all, 43 young men would start the trip with them. Nearly all were in their twenties and some, like George Shannon, were teenagers.

Since they could not carry all their food with them the explorers would often have to hunt for their food in the wilderness. Their supplies included flintlock rifles, gunpowder and metal balls as ammunition.

The Expedition Begins

In May 1804 the Lewis and Clark expedition was ready to go. They entered the Missouri River for the first of many times.

Led by Captain Clark they traveled upstream in a **keelboat** and two canoe-shaped boats. The 55-foot-long keelboat carried a square-shaped sail and at least 20 oars.

Traveling separately, Captain Lewis met them in the small French village of St. Charles. Then they continued upriver together. The group camped north of the tiny, seven-house village of La Charrette on May 25. After La Charrette, all the villages ahead would be Indian.

Council Bluffs

In August Lewis and Clark met with six chiefs to the Oto and Missouri tribes in their first **council.** They gathered on a bluff overlooking the western side of the Missouri River.

During some gift giving Lewis and Clark handed out large medals from President Jefferson that said "Peace and Friendship." This was one of the most important messages that Lewis and Clark gave to the American Indians. President Jefferson had also asked that all chiefs be invited to visit him.

After some speeches the council ended in friendship. In the future, about 25 miles below this spot, an Iowa city would be called Council Bluffs in honor of this occasion.

The First Loss

On August 20 the expedition suffered its first **casualty.** Sergeant Floyd had become suddenly

sick. After a day of extreme pain, he died, most likely of a ruptured **appendix.**

The sergeant's companions could not save him. They buried him on a hill overlooking the river. A tall monument stands there today in his honor.

Hill of the Little People

Four days later the expedition sighted a high hill standing alone on the treeless, level plain. Indians said the hill was the home of evil people 18 inches tall. All the tribes in the area stayed away from it. Armed with sharp arrows, the little humans were said to kill anyone that came near.

Captains Lewis and Clark wanted to explore this special hill called Spirit Mound, in what is now South Dakota. If they could see the little creatures, the captains would have a very interesting report to give President Jefferson.

The following morning they set out with York and about ten others. Although the hill was several miles away Clark set a fast pace, so the group reached it by noon.

The explorers climbed to its top and enjoyed the wide view of the plains and buffalo herds. They saw some animal burrows on the top but could not see the creatures.

The day was hot and everyone grew tired and thirsty. On the way back to the boats York found keeping up to be an extra struggle. In his notes, Clark wrote that York was fat and unused to walking fast. With Clark's fast pace, everyone was sure to get in better shape soon.

New Animals

In September Lewis and Clark saw some animals that were new to them. They saw acres of holes filled with furry ground animals they called barking squirrels. Today they are called prairie dogs. They saw their first pronghorn antelope and also a 45-foot-long dinosaur backbone. Earlier in the expedition they had seen buffaloes, deer, elk, coyotes, catfish and beavers.

MEETING INDIANS ALONG THE WAY

As they continued upriver the expedition met several Sioux (soo) Indian warriors. Across the plains ahead the Sioux Nation was divided into more than a dozen separate tribes. Lewis and Clark first met the Yankton Sioux in August. That meeting had gone peacefully with gift giving and peace-pipe smoking. Then the company came upon the Teton Sioux in September and had some trouble.

First the Tetons stole one of the only two horses the expedition had at the time. Then they tried to take control of the keelboat. The Tetons had several captives from the Omaha Indian tribe. These captives told the expedition that the Tetons planned to stop them from going upriver.

Lewis and Clark tried to be as friendly as they

could. They gave gifts. They attended many cere-
monies and Indian dances at the Teton **teepee**
camp. They smoked peace pipes and gave tours of
their boats. They let some of the Teton chiefs
sleep on the keelboat overnight. They ate Indian
meals including buffalo and dog meat.

Still the Tetons kept them from going. The
Tetons far outnumbered Lewis and Clark's crew
and kept their bows and arrows ready. Twice the
Tetons almost started a conflict, but on the captains' orders, the crew aimed their single-shot
guns and stood firm.

Finally one chief, named Black Buffalo, chose
to help the explorers. When many warriors sat on
the rope keeping the keelboat tied to the shore,
Black Buffalo yanked the rope away from them.
Then the sympathetic chief boarded the boat and
stayed on until the expedition crossed the Teton
territory.

The expedition soon received friendlier greet-
ings again. Early in October Lewis and Clark met
with the Arikara chiefs in council. Farther up the
river in what is now North Dakota, they met the
Mandans.

These Indians lived as farmers and grew corn,
squash, beans and other crops. Sometimes they
hunted buffalo but the more warlike tribes often
kept them out of the best hunting grounds.

Inside their wood-fenced villages the Arikaras and Mandans lived in large round-roofed houses made of willow branches, earth and straw. The structures were kept warm by fires and a hole in the center of the roofs let the smoke out.

At the councils Lewis and Clark again gave gifts, medals and speeches. They spoke of Thomas Jefferson's wish that all Indian nations live peacefully.

The Arikaras and Mandans were impressed with Lewis and Clark's show of friendship. To York and Clark's surprise the Indians were especially impressed with York, who acted out a story of being a wild animal that ate people before being tamed. He showed feats of strength and made his eyes roll. York enjoyed the joke and carried on some more. The Indian children followed him around to see what he would do next.

Fort Mandan

All the explorers enjoyed the friendliness of these Indians. As winter came near the crew created a camp nearby to survive the season of ice and snow. They built several large cabins close to a Mandan village. They called their camp Fort Mandan.

Stories about the Lewis and Clark expedition spread. During their stay several other Indian tribes, including the Hidatsa Minitaris, came to visit them. Some French fur traders in the area also offered their services to Lewis and Clark as interpreters.

Charbonneau and Sacagawea

One of these traders was Charbonneau. He knew the language of the Hidatsa Minitaris, which the others in Lewis and Clark's company found hard to speak. Through Charbonneau, Lewis and Clark met Sacagawea for the first time.

Sacagawea could help them get horses from her people, the Shoshonis, for crossing the high Rocky Mountains. Also having a woman in the expedition would show others that they were not a war party.

While staying at Fort Mandan Sacagawea gave birth to her first baby on February 11, 1805. Named Jean Baptiste by Charbonneau, the boy was called "Pomp," an Indian word for the first-born child, by Clark.

TIME TO GO

By spring, the subzero temperatures of winter were gone. In April, Lewis and Clark started the expedition on its way again. They traveled in two boats and six canoes. The keelboat was sent back to St. Louis loaded with boxes of items for President Jefferson. These items included all kinds of animal, plant and rock specimens, as well as charts, maps and gifts from the Indians.

Several men guided the keelboat, leaving 33 explorers, including the Charbonneaus, for the expedition to the Pacific Ocean.

New Lands

On the maps of the time, the land ahead was almost blank. Lewis wrote that the day they left Fort Mandan was one of the happiest moments in his life. Crossing the future states of North Dakota and Montana, Lewis wrote that "the whole face of the country was covered with herds of buffalo, elk and antelopes. . . . [They] are so gentle that we pass near them while feeding, without appearing to excite any alarm among them; and when we attract their attention, they frequently approach us more nearly to discover what we are."

Although the explorers saw no people for a long time in these lands, they still had plenty of adventures. Besides almost getting bitten by poisonous rattlesnakes there were unusual encounters with a grizzly bear and a charging buffalo.

The Grizzly Bear

The explorers began to see signs of grizzly bears in early May. They had heard grizzlies were tough to kill. They soon found out for themselves.

On May 14 six hungry explorers crept up on a giant grizzly bear. From about 80 steps away four of them fired their single-shot rifles. All shots hit. The grizzly bear charged toward them. The two other hunters fired. The shots seemed only to sting and anger the bear. It kept coming as fast as ever. Everyone ran for his life. Two of the men leaped over a 20-foot riverbank and landed in the water. The giant bear came storming at their

heels. By this time, one hunter had reloaded his gun and shot straight at the giant's head. This time the giant fell.

After enjoying a feast of bear steaks, the explorers continued on their way. Soon after this event Captain Lewis saw the immense, snow-covered Rocky Mountains for the first time. He admired their beauty, but at the same time thought they would be very hard to cross.

The Charging Buffalo

A few nights later while the tired explorers slept, a buffalo charged into their camp, stomping and crushing everything in its way. The huge animal headed straight toward the captains' tent. The sentry shouted but the buffalo came too fast. Luckily, Lewis's Newfoundland dog faced the large intruder. Barking loudly, the dog scared the big beast over to the side and away from the camp. In a second the buffalo was gone. Lewis and Clark then woke up and asked what they had missed.

Voyage Through Water

By June the expedition reached the Great Falls of Missouri. Lewis and Clark met the Shoshonis in August. Sacagawea interpreted. By the end of the month they had traded goods for 29 horses to carry their supplies over the Rocky Mountains. A

Shoshoni called Toby and his son guided them across the range to the Clearwater River.

Leaving their branded horses with the Nez Percé Indians, the explorers set off in freshly made dugout canoes for the Columbia River.

Crossing what is now Idaho, they voyaged down the Clearwater and Snake rivers and on into the big Columbia. Halfway across the future state of Washington they came to a channel of rapids that flowed between two giant rocks.

With no room to walk their canoes around the swift-moving, swirling white water, Clark took a chance and rowed ahead. Some Indians watched from high above as Clark's canoe entered the wild rapids. Luckily Clark survived and the other canoes followed. He wrote, "I was determined to pass through this. . . . We passed safe to the astonishment of all the Indians."

The Pacific Ocean

Finally, in November the canoes came close to the Pacific Ocean. Clark wrote, "Ocean in view! Oh, the joy!"

That December the expedition built a new winter camp. They called it Fort Clatsop after the Clatsop Indians.

After a rain-filled winter they set off for home in March 1806. Going back was easier. The trust-

worthy Nez Percé Indians had their horses waiting for them. When the expedition reached the Missouri River they could follow its strong current and go faster.

On the way Lewis and Clark separated to explore a wider area. On Lewis's side trip he almost got killed.

Indian Conflict

On the way across the land called Montana today, Lewis visited a western section they had skipped on the outward journey. Coming back toward the Missouri River he met a band of eight Blackfeet Sioux warriors. Other Indian tribes said they were among the most warlike in the area.

There were bound to be other bands of the Blackfeet nearby. The warriors had about 30 horses with them. Lewis had only nine men with him.

The captain gave gifts to the band and camped with them for the night.

In the morning Lewis woke up to find that the Blackfeet were stealing their rifles. One of the men, Reuben Fields, caught one thief and stabbed him with his knife. Then the band started to steal their horses too.

Without horses or rifles Lewis and his party could easily starve or be killed in the wilderness.

Captain Lewis drew his pistol and fired at a Black-foot. The Indian fired his rifle back. The rifle shot just missed Lewis's head. Lewis's shot had hit the Blackfoot in the stomach.

The band fled. They left the weapons and almost half their 30 horses. In case the Blackfeet were planning to return in a war party of greater numbers, Lewis and his men raced their horses for a hundred miles through the day and night.

Clark enjoyed an easier time. His group voyaged along the Yellowstone River in what is now southern Montana. Carving his name on some stones to show where he'd explored, he came to a tall, giant rock that especially pleased him.

He named the towering rock after Sacagawea's son. It is called Pompey's Pillar. Guarded carefully with a grill and glass, Clark's large signature can still be seen today.

◆◆◆◆◆◆◆◆◆◆◆◆◆◆

LEWIS AND CLARK RETURN!

In August Lewis and Clark safely grouped together again at the Missouri River. Moving swiftly with the current they reached the tiny village of La Charrette on September 20. The next day they came to St. Charles. Two days later, on September 23, the expedition arrived in St. Louis. The explorers were eagerly welcomed by the townspeople.

Except for one member everyone had lived through the entire expedition. Sergeant Floyd had been the only casualty.

The expedition covered more than 7,000 miles of travel. The U.S. Congress awarded double pay to every expedition member and large tracts of open land to Lewis and Clark.

Lewis was made the governor of the Louisiana Territory. After Lewis died in 1809 Clark was soon made the governor and also the Superintendent of Indian Affairs. Clark married and eventually had five children. In honor of his friend, he named his first son Meriwether Lewis Clark.

Eventually Clark freed York, an uncommon act for a Southerner in those times. Some say York went to live as a respected chief among the Crow tribe. Sacagawea returned to the Shoshonis. Pomp, or Jean Baptiste, returned to the Shoshonis as a grown man after living with Clark for a while and visiting Europe for five years. Clark died in 1838.

Lewis and Clark Inspire Others

Lewis and Clark's efforts gave Americans more knowledge about the people and wildlife of this beautiful land. They also showed that people of various **cultures** could be friends if they were careful and considerate. Like other great explorers, Lewis and Clark opened the minds of others to a wider world.

GLOSSARY

appendix—An outgrowth inside the body at the beginning of the large intestine.

cascades—One or more waterfalls with rippling folds that shimmer or sparkle.

casualty—A serious or fatal accident.

colonial—A land that is controlled by another country.

council—A meeting for consultation or discussion.

cultures—The skills, customs and beliefs of a group of people.

elk—A large deer with broad antlers.

expedition—A journey undertaken for scientific purposes or the group of people undertaking such a trip.

interpreter—One who translates one language to another language.

keelboat—A large, shallow freight boat with an extra strip of wood along its bottom.

ravine—A long, narrow, steep-sided ditch that is usually worn away by running water.

scout—One who explores an area in advance of others, to obtain information.

teepee—A cone-shaped American Indian tent of animal skins.

INDEX